MY LOVE WAS BLIND

By La Wanda Marrero

Published by Unstoppable Publishing company, USA

ISBN: 978-1-963917-00-0 (sc)
ISBN: 978-1-963917-01-7 (hc)
ISBN: 978-1-963917-02-4 (e)

Library of Congress Control Number: 2024903860

TABLE OF CONTENTS

Introduction
Dedication

INTRODUCTION

This book evolved as I committed myself to a five-thousand-word count in my co-authored book *Blinded Love*. Unconsciously I poured myself into the story and when the contents reached the paper it flowed into over eighty-thousand words of past loves and the root that lies beneath my imagination. God revealed me to me the inner truth and the debts of his salvation for me. I was unknowing guilty, ignorant to understanding how I contributed but God shined His light in me, and my eyes were open to My Love was Blind.

DEDICATION

I dedicate this chapter to the people in my life that encourage me to keep going. Such as Julie Whitten, Auntie Caroline, The Dings, my children and grands, my church family, Mama Marie who now rest in peacefully in the universe, my auntie social work team, Harriet, Carrie, Delo, Dollie, and especially my mom, Brenda Fayne, my butterfly who has gone on to be with the Lord, and to you reader. The journey is hard and continuous, but I carry the spirit of your Love and belief in me.

To all my fist flash lovers taking pleasure in the abusive demise of breaking me down physically, emotionally, and spiritually you have contributed to the core of my value system. I recognize who I am and to whom I belong. I was born purposely to the world ,even before I knew I had the Lord's protection. I remember telling my husband, Vince not an abuser but a different type of heartache. He opened my eyes and heart to see love. Learn more about his in my book, "Alice N Crackland, that no matter what happened in our marriage from Jesus I came and to Jesus I shall always return. I also told him he would see Jesus in my eyes one day and both came to pass. Forgiveness has happened for us all. I learned and grew as I reflect on my expectation of past relationships being the source to my needs rather than depending on God. I now believe it I've always had a relationship with the Lord but didn't understand it because I was leaning on my own understanding and not getting biblically taught. My earliest memories of reading were with my grandma Bonner I was very young after her death it was scattered. The connections we made in our relationships to one another were damaged childhood souls leaning in trapped adult addictions, trauma, and life mirages with no understanding about God, repentance, and holiness.

Also, to Chicago my heart beats and the waters run deep with thoughts of You.

I'm grateful I have been found and filled with God's love. I am also grateful that I had an opportunity to revisit the people in blinded relationships and make amends given peace to them and myself. To God be the glory!

CHAPTER ONE

Stained Scars & Warranted Wounds

I often hear your skin is so beautiful and you are so photogenic. My response is, "it must be Jesus." I heard a speaker say on zoom once we are all usually busy looking at ourselves while zooming. Her words startled my attention she was right especially in my case. Selfconfidence had me practice turning my face to hide my black eyes, asking myself if others could see them? While scanning me I also learned that I wasn't the only behavioral bizarreness on zoom. There is much effort in zoom etic and sometimes is often forgotten that the camera is on. I was not alone. Thankfully so! The reflection I see when I look in the mirror are the stained scars and warranted wounds. I was defending myself in yesterday's battle. There were strategic and impulsive attacks from my end and a fear-based perception of what ifs. I was in search of love, it felt like the right circumstances in all the wrong places, unbe knowing to me. Blinded love got me raccoon blacken eyes, smashed face, cracked head, busted lips, tossed, body bruising, and emotional distraught. By the end of this book, you the reader; will be able to point out many other defaults and disturbing behaviors. As I bear the reality of my life and experiences so vividly.

My prayer without self-judgment is that you the reader pray for me as I do for you.

For those who have read my work and newcomers. I would like to refresh my Phrase *Pen & pad moment!* When you read this phrase pay close attention because most likely it's something that is life defining. It may or may not be similar to the identifiable experiences of others. It may possibly connect to a desire, interest, and/or lust of the flesh. There lies a lesson to bare within this chapter. I guarantee correlation and soundness will prevail. It's about learning and applying knowledge how to meditate, negotiate, and be mindful of people places and things in one's surroundings and what one deposits into the universe. What you input is your output. "We get to choose we can react or interact. "Evolving is progressive over time and working on ourselves is a difficult process but it is necessary. Keep going! *Pen & pad moment!* My struggles with self-esteem, abuse and developmental issues began long before I got into consensual relationships. As a child a wrong suitor my uncle, displayed an inappropriate attraction to me by molesting me. My earliest aged memories were combined with two examples of male relationships, sexual violation and watching my mother get beat down. What I witnessed took prevalence in my life. I stood there watching my mama pinned by her aggressors' control. My eyes were pierced with fear as I watched him tower over her with numerous hits to her face, he was dark, and he seem to be so tall bam/smack all I could do was weep. I was too stunned to turn away. Because this was my first recollection of war in marriage by way of a fist, I generally avoided dark skinned men. I also sized a guy up by trying to make sure I was a little taller than him just in case I might have to take him down.

Both in the Lou and Cali my childhood thoughts and actions regarding relationships were guarded I was deeply rooted to watching fist face pounding, from the men in my family. It seemed to happen often especially at family functions. There was also hoarding and anger points of separation. My members of my family as Madea says, "keeps a piece of steal," even back then and today. I used to ask why but after a previous trip to St. Louis on the day of my mama, Brenda's repass my aunt, niece, daughters, and granddaughter were bystanders in a near shoot out. We got out answer and if you been to the Lou, you know why to. The kids keep their water pistols ready to. I also give recognition during family gatherings sometimes hot buttons get pushed! I was mortified as a child and even when I saw it or participated in this behavior as an adult. With these examples what kind of healthy marriage could I possibly imagine and how would it become a reality. Watching them grown folks' battles I adapted to battling and being battered I was a wide open, a nurtured field to be an abuser or abused. Sometimes I still get flashbacks from my own punch-bag experiences. This was my beginning of normality in adult intimate interactions. There were healthier or should I say lasting marriages in my family, but I didn't grow up around those, I learned of them later in life.

CHAPTER TWO

Profound Humiliation

In my younger days I lived in survival mode lacking the ability to utilize appropriate coping skills, I did use my coping mechanisms though. A coping mechanism from my perspective is based on my experiential knowledge and was not healthy or productive choice for me. I had outrageousness reactions to pain and blinded love situations among other things. It took me many adult years by way of applying my master's degree education and the blood of Jesus to grasp the concept of a coping skill. With many failed practices I learned how to interact rather than react this was much more appropriate, acceptable, and calming. I then chose to learn and apply more coping skills in my life that were realistic and attainable. Such as deep breathing, praying, fasting, taking time to listen, process without rushing, attending spiritual functions, role-play positive interactions; and continuous conversation with Jesus helps me to intercede and make it through.

I often use a version of Gestalt empty chair technique by practicing saying what I want to say versus what I am going to say. So when I see the person I have worked out the emotional reactivity hopefully, and can address or respond with a form of "the turning of cheek." Prayerfully not relying on my own understanding but what the word of God tells me to do or say or not. I'm getting better at it. Thankfully so!

A male Elder seemed to be eye piercing at me at church as he approached me making meaningless chit chat, he asked me about the darkness around my eyes. I got that mortified feeling I knew all to well. I scrambled for an explanation that wasn't as embarrassing and shameful as the truth. I don't think he was trying to be insensitive sometimes other people's curiosity is an invitation for things like that to happen. My thought was what would be more tolerant than the truth? After my pause I said, "getting punched in the face repeatedly has its side effects." As I gave him a slighted grin. He nodded his head as in agreement and with urgency and deterred his attention elsewhere. With much effort I practice telling myself this is to remind me of what God has done for me and not to let my emotions be over ran with the past of who and what I had been through. If I do, utilize it find meaning and make it purposeful. It is a humbling and sometimes an uncoiled situation, but it helps when I get a little puffed up or misguided about what I don't have, or forgetful of who God is.

I remember this one Friday, Holy Ghost night and I was at choir rehearsal. I had been saved and rooted in Christ for a few years. I was just singing my heartfelt song glorifying the Lord with volume and gladness. This woman walked right up to the altar and said, "I remember you! You used to be out there on Octavia Street." My first reaction was one of humiliation and of course mortification. Her words were heard even over the music. It was profound, but then the light of deliverance overshadowed me and where God had brought me from kicked in. I hugged her and praised the Lord in song and danced rejoicing with my whole heart that night. My voice was so hoarse I could barely speak the next day. I was no longer that same person. My praise wasn't about hiding who I was, where I've been, or the things I've done but testifying about God's business in my life. This was one of my many lessons to come on how to love somebody beyond what they say or do. This is not easy for me but for restored peace I refocus on my commitment to the Lord, my confession, and the baptism of me rising in the newness of life and leaving the old La Wanda at the bottom of the pool. So, it is no longer me that lives, but it is Christ that lives through and in me. Sometimes my efforts cause me isolation and timeouts because in my flesh, "I just wanna get em back."

I have found within myself to passively hold grudges from yesterday against the things that men have done to me or what I did to them. Stating this important for me because not only is yesterday gone but so are those old emotional relationships baggage and my preoccupied thoughts.

My synergy impacts what I attract and input in the universe. I am learning to be more in tune with myself. Focus on self-love, selfappreciation, and being my own hero. Thanks to my friend Chicago you will read about him later. No more gravitation to emptiness or unconscious self-punishment in relationships. Too often I've been led by my attraction and my body lustfulness rather than my suitor's checklist. I have failed continually in making the wrong choices about men by getting myself quickly involved. Why does La Wanda say ordo this? A lying moment is a familiar Safety. I have three different baby daddies and a questionable fourth. It wasn't that I was sleeping with a lot of different men during those baby making years. I wholeheartedly was committed to making those relationships and my family work. Self-sacrificing did not look or feel good on me or the kids. I didn't even know who I was in those broken relationships and the lying moment had worn off. I was caught up in my sensual and emotional flesh feelings. That's my story and I'm sticking to it. I can now proclaim happiness, not joy for what I went through. However, if it had not been for those faced unhappy situations, this would be a sad story rather than a victorious testimony.

CHAPTER THREE

Sacrificially Love Tracking My Loves

I believed in my creativity and specialness in matters of the heart. They were concrete and solid in my opinion. I now understand happy is a transitional happening event, what makes me happy can also make me unhappy. No one can make me happy, and it is unfair to give someone such a taxed position for my responsibility. My sacrificial love was not the same as unconditional love and will never be the source of my joy, but the misery of my soul.

I gotta truthfully admit even at this stage in my life, although I have forgiven battled relationships, I still make little comments that I should not make about my blinded loved ones. Particularly for the sake of the offspring, I talked to myself about it asking why? I believe a sensitive subject and reflective memory comes up and I have a triggering reactive flashback. I'm consciously working on those little triggers reminding myself to just appreciate what I've learned and who I have become through situational experiences. I fear for those who don't grasp that masculinity doesn't mean swinging fist, possessiveness, mind control to stand your ground as a man or woman. Thankfully so! It is my hope by the end of this book I will wear my afflictions like a badge of honor not hiding behind the fear of thoughts and yesterday's oppression. Rejection has its limits, but domestic violence and partner intimacy violence can be endless and deadly.

Tracking my loves, I learned God was always with me, no matter what, even when I couldn't hear or understand what He was saying to me. Mama Marie used to tell me I had backwards thinking, and I understand the more our matured. The core of my trust in selfjudgment and self-value stems from my early start in childhood dysfunction. I was attracted to what was on the outside rather than the inside truth of men and life's situation which ultimately   escalated from harsh words and putdowns to a pow, face punch, slap, kick, fist push, and penis play of repetitive cycles of broken blindness in loves; each taking a bite out of my soul and chipping away at the core of my existence. By the grace of God, "I made it through." Thankfully so!

I was twelve years old. I believe my feelings surfaced regarding rejection after a slightly older boy named Roy, who I met on a summer vacation trip home to the Lou. I can't remember any details about how I met him. My birth mom meant no intentional harm. She had given me this very sexy purple teddy. I don't think she knew I was wearing it on the side of the house for Roy though. To my recollection there was a little fumbling but no sexual activity. *I paused here, a flash the Lord is always protected and sheltered me.* The clueless of danger and neediness. I'll talk more about it a little bit.

I remember I was in the hospital, but I don't remember why. I used that hospital bedside rotary phone. You know the old-fashioned kind with the rotary holes if you made a mistake you had to start all over again. I called Roy's phone number over and over again with repetitive momentum, but he never answered my calls! I learned a whole lot about my emotions that summer. But one thing was consistent and is still true forty years later. *I was the flying nun.* Since my early childhood trauma, the Lord has given me the ability to be an eagle and soar above my circumstances. Thankfully so! On the outside in order to save face, not show shame or defeat of my real colors I learned to instinctively how to cope with those newfound feelings of rejection. I acted like it didn't bother me by not mentioning it. The Simmons family famous, "fake it to you make it!" are until the pain subsided. I pocket stored it into my tormented spirit and body base memory. In my imperfection unfortunately my side effect was to insert hurt and rejection inwardly, devaluing that I had purpose and I was loved which leads to a depressive hole. I've never known such love as I receive from the Lord though he made me whole. I don't see or feel about Him as I've known men.

God's masculinity is hidden in his unconditional love for me. God presents himself gentle but firm as a dove in my life situations. Sometimes in my rebellious and stubbornness I don't want to or I'm not ready to experience certain things about myself even knowing it's going to take me higher in the Lord. God still reaches for me. Sometimes is difficult to pray for myself "thank God, The Lord has His ways." And I am Thankfully so! He gets in! His love is so powerful, and I need that peace that he restores unto me. I let Him in! *Back to the flash pause, "The Lord has always protected and sheltered me."* This is not a boast in me and in my ability. "To God be the glory!" I can only say my heavenly Father and keeper of my soul knows not just me but us and our needs.

After I attended a wedding in Las Vegas. By the way contrary to popular opinion. *"What's Lays in Vegas don't stay in Vegas it beats you home."* I don't know if it was at my worst, but it certainly was one of the worst. What I do know is I was actively working at being my worst. I can't tell you if I was feeling sorry for myself or just plain hurt. I had recently published my first book and of course it was a difficult digestion and exposition of family business, there was quite a bit of backlash that crossed my path. Rightfully so!

The writing of *Alice N Crackland* was not my idea it was given to me by God. I promise you I wasn't that smart to envision such a book. Alice, *me* overshadowed coupled with the drugs, my mind and brain having notorious conversations with one another and a lot of conflicting dos and don'ts, I had lost it. God came and got me. I had heard he answered prayer and I know it to be true. The problem is I thought he would answer according to my imagination rather than his expectation. I came to be joyful for the times he ignored my wants but never my needs. Although I know I was not living right I cried out and one day He showed up and my deliverance was undeniable afoot.

I intentionally tried to cliff jump out of the Palm of God's hand during that Vegas trip. I remember His ANGER with me. I got a shivering body flashback just writing about it for the second time, or it could have been the air conditioner; it is definitely something I can't forget. Throughout my life even before I understood about holiness the Lord has gotten me out and brought me through unsavory situations. Some I created some I stumbled into. It has been more than a few occasions where I was persistent in trying to give myself to someone sexually or flirting with danger. More times than not my plans were derailed and thankfully so! There are detailed readable facts also in my book *Alice N Crackland.*

My unique perception of my anxious activity during these times were not reality but broken images and my damaged thought life hardwiring. I could have said, "let's blame it on the alcohol," using that as my state of being. The truth is I had been in a full-on Drunken awake stupor unsafely in rigorous search of a lying moment. "Why you ask?" From the beginning of time, it was my impulsive go to hidden painful coping strategic coping mechanism for selfpunishment, familiarity, and validation. I had not yet learned new skills to cope with the pain rather than self-sabotage. Familiarity good or bad has some rationalization of SAFETY.

My confession is that I have often made choices that I thank God it didn't turn out like I planned. He once even, allowed me to be arrested overnight while I was wearing a white and black pinstripe outfit. He matched the circumstances to my outfit. Deservedly so! That night in jail probably saved me once again and kept me from dying being the cliff diver that I am. I want you the reader to really know yourself and be honest even if you have to seek help from a professional do it. Yes, I lay my burdens on the alter however I learned to tap into skills that lay dormant inside myself as a professional. What to do when the taunting returned to rebuke that torture without reaching for familiarity but embracing the new safeness without the attachment of self-destruction.

Sometimes I could become so out of control, overwhelmed by those familiar spirits that came to taunt me into giving up on Jesus. I am just going to be honest there are things that I will not talk to my pastor or no other pastor about.

I have learned this. My dust doesn't need to float around in their head besides they might not have the skills needed and that is pressure. I wanna be able to hold my head up high not have wondering thoughts about my dirt when I'm in the presence of the Pastor.

I would become so confused in the waiting for change. I couldn't and wouldn't look at the possibility of accountability for my actions. I was compelled to reach into yesterday for a coping mechanism. Prayer is hard to foresee in hardships. Sometimes it can take a while to manifest even though the healing is instant. I practice walking in it by faith as the well-known slogan states, "God may not be there when you want Him to be, but He is always right on time." I woke up grateful that through my attempts God had kept me intact. But I was guilty! I confess that guilt and sin! Damned unholy roots! Thank the Lord the correlation between holiness and sin is the blood of Jesus.

Pen & pad moment! I lived my life in the basement of emptiness of my perversion after that Las Vegas night as I set on the plane. I believe the flight home might have even been rocky as well, calling for me to ask God for his mercy and grace while traveling to safety. I knew judgment was on me after that night. I made it home safely, however there were no usual at ease benefits and provisions I normally get supplied. Nobody to pick me up from the airport because of car trouble, no available cabs parked at the Bart station, and back then there was no Uber or Lyft car services. Both suitcases and I struggled making it to the house. I had such a hard time getting home it crossed my mind to leave those bags on the street several times, but I prevailed taking my punishment with my big girl draws on. I was well aware of the difference in God's usual communication and the meaning of my unanswered calls for transportation help.

This had been the second time in my life I knowingly felt that kind of anger from God against me. His wrath overshadowed my entire being and he neither sought nor had fellowship with me not even by my invitation for a justified period of time.

The first noticed unforeseen God's ANGER toward me was my involved role in the death of a homeless man named, TU. I'll address this later in another chapter. *Fresh revelation* given to me while writing this regarding God's angry side. Why anger but not rejection? Because this was in the lesson plan for me. The only time self-sacrificing was the appropriate and accepting offering. "I connected some dots such as no matter what, I will never need man's validation only God's and some lost parts of me returned unto me. "My Jesus, My Lord, my father you have been more than merciful to me, thank you!"

CHAPTER FOUR

Blinded Love

Pen & pad moment! At age sixteen I experienced a sexual traumatic event dating Carlo, an ex-boyfriend. He grew to become quite controlling and aggressive which was not a part of his original character when we began as a couple. It is possible I didn't notice *blinded love.* He was my first real love, and I was his practice doll dummy, "it happens." Before him there was BC. I met BC in middle school we became sort of boyfriend girlfriend after we fought each other. It was a pretty huge fight. It happened within the first few days of me arriving at a new school in a new town, Sausalito. I was challenged to or shall we say dared to go to the Marin City tunnel to fight him. He was not no little boy neither I can't even remember why, but back then boys didn't know how to say I like you it was complicated. They teased and taunted. I had to hide my little girl *Alice* cry from mama Marie when I called home for permission to stay after school and make friends. I really wanted to say please come and get me, but I knew it would make it worse if I backed down. Things seemed to be different with this black dominated school than the one I attended in Fresno which was primarily white cultured.

In shivery I walked to that tunnel wearing my favorite multicolor shirt. I felt anxious hairs on the back of my neck as BC walked in back of me. The flying nun soared above my circumstances of fear and his too big to be in my grade. I coached myself to be brave and let the element of surprise make me the victor. I turned and launched out into the deep swinging, punching, weaving, kicking, and wobbling my arms in circular overhead motions with thrusting force. The crowds were yelling and cheering it on. BC was caught off guard and a bit mortified. He had no expectation of how the fight was going to go down. But I don't think he thought it through. I was not like the girls he was accustomed to I was one of the Simmons girls. As I reflect back, we had a dinner date as adults when I lived in Vallejo, but he was like a young old Christian man and scared of me. He received an urgent text followed by a return call and he left without eating dinner. To my recollection as kids there was some fumbling behind the school but nothing more.

Now handsome Carlo who pursued my attention until I gave it to him and other parts of myself. He quickly lost entrance. This is something young girls learn early we don't expect it. Somehow, we learn to believe in the relationship romanticizing the façade until the realness moment appears. It showed up relatively quickly especially since Carlo was cute, tall, and in a band. The ladies liked that and I'm sure he adored the attention. He was young. He could've been upset that he got fired from the band because of our drama and our notoriety and bad public experiences regarding him turning key holes with more than just me. Even with a girl who lived in the same apartment complex as him. Of course, I took it as rejection he was done with me but had a jealousy issue regarding my relationship choices with others.

Carlo got caught cheating, he didn't want me but didn't want nobody else to have me neither. I found a variety of posed, pictures of girls in the car and lined them all up to take note of his expression. I didn't like his response when I questioned him about it. Our time together grew awkward and scarce. I guess one day he was probably looking for me in Marin City and noticed my car was parked at Pretty Boy's house. I gave him that nickname and it definitely fit him and his swag. Pretty Boy was a high school glitch we weren't really lovers although he was interested. I learned this after we had taken a high school sex education class together and my brother Deely. The two of them were the tightest of friends and Deely wanted me to consider dating Pretty Boy. Since it was a spoken break up with Carlo, I gave Pretty Boy a chance to show me his intentions for my body. He had a nice package, but it somehow always felt awkward or if we were trying to force it with each other. Sex was not the true nature of our friendship.

Carlo knocked on Pretty Boy's door unexpectedly. In order to keep it from getting ugly I went with him. We ended up having to consensual sex but this time it was something different happened he hurt me, he was rough. You would think

I would not see him again but that wasn't the case. It was the last time we had sex though. I learned that I had a brain tumor after making inquiries about my weight gain. I was scheduled to have brain surgery shortly after prom. Carlos was supposed to be my prom date. Marie was at a conference or something out of town but before she left, she had assisted with the items I needed for prom. Prom night with Carlo was the absolute worst night of my young life. The arguing and disconnect it was an early uneventful evening I should have let Pretty Boy take me. We continued to be friends over the years as our separate lives evolved. Even after Carlo knew I had brain surgery he didn't check on me or come and see me except once and that is because he needed some money. The last time I saw him it was a stormed event. I found the house and girl's car Carlo was driving. It turned into a major altercation I ended up breaking every one of those windows and put holes in the tires, everything was broken "Look up nigga it's over I got you! Click" Unfortunately he did not get to see me in God's glory.

Disco queen *1978* eighteen, some people have a good get in the door technique but lack in their follow through. I first met Charles Preston Jefferson Sr. father of my firstborn son, Charles Preston Jefferson Jr., and oldest daughter at the Palladium club in San Francisco California. A *lying moment* escalated quickly between us.

I was desperate to leave home after recovering from brain surgery My present understanding, it wasn't so much of wanting to leave home I was merely broken on the inside. I had never talked about my childhood sexual trauma with Marie. I just couldn't find the words to explain my damaged heart that revealed my pain the older I got. How could I tell her those kind of things about the people she loved?

I packed my stuff in that old gangster Vox wagon and set out for the world to be with Charles without knowing anything about him, except he was the first guy to perform oral sex on me instant *blinded love.* I soon got the opportunity to meet him in his exactness along with his intravenous drug shooting self. One day he rolled up a sleeve, tied something around his arm, patted it and shot a needle in his arms. He then told me I might as well know that he sold pills to. Suddenly it was formatted in my mind. I had moved from Sausalito to sixth St. I was wowed but, in my stubbornness, I vowed to never shoot no drugs and to make this living arrangement work. During the writing of this I noticed a pattern when I needed to move or do something different, I often made sacrifices and put up with circumstance that were neither productive nor healthy for me.

I shockingly got pregnant shortly after we got together. The doctors had told me previously that I probably would not be able to conceive because of the brain tumor. Boy where they wrong. Junior was born early I lived in distress partnered with Charles. My premature son had pulmonary issues and needed a small amount of oxygen. I was with Junior every day for four months dressing him, learning about the machine functions, and caretaking him. Junior died of crib death after coming home from a very long four-month hospital stay. He was found by Charles in his white bassinet crib. In my heart my life perished. Although Marie had much disappointment in me and my behaviors her love for me never wilted. She took care of me and the cost of Juniors funeral. She even tried to get me to come home but I repaid her kindness with rejection, to do so. I just couldn't, I thinks she took it personal, but it wasn't. I still couldn't sort out my childhood hurtful feelings. Marie was always there when I needed her right up until she was done with her codependency phase of life. Thank God, "I'm a mother of many daughters so I do understand the pain of mourning to the morning."

There is no superhero insurance for blinded love. Tag you are it. I felt pain and unknowingly exercised hurting others. I inserted my wonderful self into the lives of men with the expectation that my love and my babies had to be enough. It was my imaginary mindset of happy ever after especially once I had children. I used my emotional abuse to solicit the attention of men. My imagination told me family was security, but it turned out not to be safe. Somewhere I missed the point. Marie used to also say, "don't cast your pearls before swine." Somehow, I couldn't tell the difference my pearls were stolen a long time ago with malice intent and my innocence discarded. I played my role the one I was taught. I can relate being abused and an abuser as well; I learned *to give it and to get it.* I did should have left after Charles Jr. died. Marie reached for me but in my blind ignorance I stayed, in time the potential fatality of our relationship rang true.

In the relationship with Charles, I soon recognized my weaknesses that laid within me. I had given energy and effort, but anguish and heartbreak were what I received in return. I got more deeply into addiction after the death of Junior. The night he died I even snorted heroin, but I didn't like the feeling, nodding, or the throw up after I ingested it. I never snorted it again, but mountains of Cocaine would soon be the new thing. My only source to plug into was the Lord Jesus without any understanding of what that meant, I was connected to Him, and the people, places, or things he placed in my path. I soon came to learn relationship with this man had no future. *That it was an M & M strike!*

I became pregnant for a second time. This time giving birth to a healthy beautiful baby girl. I also experienced distress during this pregnancy of his in and out of jail, womanizing, and drug use. The relationship grew more toxic daily cuddled with his wanting to control me. In order to surpass what he was or not doing he grew aggressive and combative. The hitting and the degrading started, and I knew there was not future in this. Marie had voiced her concern after I had answered her question, he was good enough to have a baby for but certainly not good enough to marry.

I strategically waited to use his anger and aggressiveness towards me to make an exit plan for me and my daughter. It proved to be an unfair burden to work hard toward loving someone more than I loved myself. His love hurt like an *M & M bite*, it's came with sexually transmitted diseases, slaps, punches, putdowns, no finance or perks, starvation, kicks, and his heroin drug use. I was also gifted a nice nasty mother-in-law who reaped of pain herself. Charles once told me he was living with a grandma out of town as a kid and this lady knocked on the door. He went to the screen door. He said, " Grandma there's a lady at the door." When Charles opened the door, the woman slapped his face and said, "I ain't no lady I'm your mama." I learned all this shortly after my hasty "set off for the world's life move-in adventure with him. "Yet I still didn't swallow my pride and take my ass home though." Charles grew dangerous. I guess I reminded him of what he should be able to do and was he wasn't doing, sometimes I did not have to do or say anything. After he returned home from his binges, he would be broke, ashamed, and get agitated with himself but take it out on me.

Mother's Day was coming, and people kept asking what I was going to do for myself my response, " I am going to give myself the present of freedom." An opportunity prevailed, after a long and drawn-out day of fighting with Charles going back and forth, I decided to go to the store to purchase something for dinner. While out I plotted our exit plan to be ready. I left our daughter with him so that I could get back to the house quickly.

When I returned, I felt eerie the lights were off, I picked up the baby noticing it seemed to be some dark areas around the front of her mouth and she was quiet. Charles and I ended up in another argument this time he pulled out a huge knife. "Now where did that suddenly come from and how long has it been there?" OH, MY LORD! I just figured this out as I'm writing. "God showed up again and took care of me;" I have been blind as a wheel within a wheel. "Please forgive me." I guess being a social worker was always a calming trait lying dormant in me. Today I realize it wasn't my skills but God's grace. He took what was hidden on the inside me the MSW (Master of Social Work). Marie and her team of top-of-the-line Black social workers instilled in me to reach for my safety place for comfort. For me that was being the flying nun *Alice childhood survival techniques* was to search for a way to soar above my circumstances. This also created mild alternate personality transitions like Chickee to stand in and assist me with the courage to do so. I used it all to talk him down!

Charles stabbed that knife into the dresser with such thrust that it stood straight up wobbling. "You know that lump you get in your throat when your think-fast fight or flight reflex kicks-in?" I learned to be quiet, humbled, and reassuring to whatever he said or needed. I stroked his eagle, praised his thoughts anything to cool those raging waters. I even laid down beside him not expecting to nap. I woke up to him punching me so hard in my face that my nose bled. He was asking me, "what I was thinking about?" This was the opportunity I had been waiting for to scat out. I applied forced pressure on my nose disguised as holding and sobbing. This startled him and made my nose bleed worse. I now realize Charles had a heart in that chest his actions showed panicked fear not all abusers call the ambulance. Upon the arrival of help I took the time to stuff my daughters clothes in my bag while he let the paramedics in. I refused to let anyone hold my baby. I told them I was not letting her go. Charles was outside in the waiting room. I made a call to my aunt and told her my intentions to leave asking her to pick me and my daughter up at the hospital. After receiving treatment, I walked to the back of the hospital in hopes that we could just slip out the back door to the parking lot but when we got to the back of the hospital Charles was standing there. There was a very long corridor from the back of the hospital to the parking lot. I made meaningless chit chat and when I arrived at the end of the corridor where the armed police where I looked at Charles,

"You know I'm not going back?" I left him from the hospital and never returned except to pick up the rest of my baby's items.

I spent many years trying to get Charles to visit our daughter. I ongoingly opened the door for him to have a relationship with her but he didn't step through it. He was caught up in his lifestyle and I had moved on it never happened. Our daughter did have some time to time with his mother and his siblings. Twelve years later Charles was living with his mother. At their request I took our daughter to see them. I overheard him telling someone loudly that he had AIDS from his own mouth I understood that he wanted to make an amends. I took our daughter to see him every day for six months at his home. She sang at his funeral when he died. In the end he saw the glory of God in me and her.

CHAPTER FIVE

Steet Life Dare to Do

Twenty-one years old welcome to official adulthood and the old man dares. Red Cap was probably the most unorthodox relationship that I ever had he certainly was oldest man I dated. I had two-daughters for him. He was thirty-one years my senior. I got with this man on a birthday dare from my sister-cuz Yolo. She told me he liked me and asked about me. We were young and did crazy stuff like that all the time. The dare conspired of going over saying hello and get him to make a date with me. I did go over I already had a date that night with the most boring guy. I was excited when that date ended by midnight, I had guessed the end time of that date just right. I was anxious to get back to the bar to see if the old man had that bottle of champagne he promised. I hooked up with him, after a night of bliss and blind drunkenness I was off and running into the next lying moment lasting for years with babies for benefits.

During those rounds the table smoke outs I learned that Redcap had been a pimp in his earlier years riding in the crew with Filmore Slim. In those days they called him Broham Sam. His pimping days where supposedly over and he was a coke dealer. Our relationship was totally different he was the opposite with me. He never approached me in that manner about booty sales, but he did increase my knowledge about the drug game. I could tell from his historical accounts of his life he didn't respect women very much yet there I was. I furthered his taught information with what I knew already. I had become a partner with a girlfriend in packaging and bar sales of cocaine packages after me and Charles split. When I got involved with Red Cap I intentionally dummied up. I was running my own after-hours distribution while he was at work as Ms. Cap. I was respected I learned enough about the business to run it on the streets and without him if necessary.

There were a few issues though it was in the 80's when women weren't drug dealers but whores. I needed his permission to deal with the connects if he said no that didn't stop me. I used that MSW on the connects.

One time when Redcap found out after getting out of jail the connect was dealing with me without his permission. He was upset but he had no reason to be there was money on his books, I had bought him a new pair of glasses, and there was plenty of product to keep us floating. We were participating in one of our round table smoke marathons. He approached me as if he was going to hit me my survival mode kicked-in and I pulled his coat over his head flipping him over the bed. He never tried that sh..t again.

On a fluke I soon learned Redcap was involved with other women. It was a Xmas season the girls and me were staying in Sausalito with Marie. I guess this was one of those times I did allow her to help me. Redcap had previously given me money to get the girls raingear and they were fitted from head to toe. We caught a bus into San Francisco to surprise him. When me and my babies knocked on his door, I got the surprise. There was this straggly looking old white woman there and she was wearing the robe I bought him for Xmas. I lost it, "I am not going to be the only one hurt," I call this a contact visit I punched her in her face so hard as he sped walk behind me and the children as we headed for the elevator. The children and I were silent on the way home. Sad my girls witnessing my wrath stuck rage.

I later learned from him that I broke her jaw and that's how she made her money. *I had no remorse!*

Redcap had a straight job working for Pac bell I didn't even know he had other women. His slogan became, "I'm gone pimp white girls and sale dope to they tell me I can't," *meaning the police,* "who was this old nigga trying to be and what role had I taken?" I know he would disappear for hours claiming he was out copping. I figured out he was sitting up somewhere get it in. Another incident happened where he called me to come and pick up some money and go to jail to bail out this young white girl. Angered with him I did it. I walked into the bail bondsman office, and he definitely knew I was livid the way I threw that money down. But now it was time to plot, scheme, and cheat my way right out of the relationship. My edged childhood roughness for the safety of *Alice* was on alert and my Chickee and JaRasta personality showed up rescuing me and gave me the false courage. *Hook and crook headed his way.*

Redcap was in and out of jail a lot always getting his hotel doors kicked in by the police. I somehow through the grace of God was either on my way or leaving when he got raided. Thankfully so.

My chosen path had gotten busted on the street for direct sales to the police three times. My bout with selling drugs was over. I got me a job in Churches chicken and was quite satisfied with my salary and freedom. I remember one time while Redcap was in locked up, he wanted me to go to this hotel room. He had hidden a package there in a suitcase and the hotel manager agreed to hold the suitcase until I picked it up. What Redcap failed to understand unlike him I was no longer in the cash and carry business. I still was an addict with an appetite though. I went to the hotel I found the suitcase I unlocked it and there it was right there stuffed in the tube sock just like he said. I don't know what he thought I was not going back to selling dope and secondly how could I hold onto dope for an extended time. I smoked it all and told him I didn't find it. He knew I was lying but I didn't care *Payback.* I had made up my mind that I was going to get him back for those white girl' stunts and the way to get him was through his pockets. He was so focused on trying to please me like I was some kind of bottom chick that he was careless. He was giving me stacks of money and dope and I was just giving his stuff away. This pushed him to work harder and take penitentiary chances and he did. I don't know why I was so mad at him I had a side piece, her man Stan long before me and Redcap ever got together. I saw Stan monthly on my weekends away to my play auntie No's house. Stan was her brother. Once again it was complicated. It was nothing serious Stan was never abusive. He was a pimp not my pimp but my lover. We were always so hot for each other's body and stimulating topic discussions. We had no and didn't want any expectation from one another. It was mutual respect and carpet burns. We eventually grew tired of our romantic interlude. His girlfriend had their baby and Me and her man Stand went our separate ways. There were some thoughts rather the daughter I had during that season was his or Red Caps. My decision was to let it be. I had no intention of being another baby mama notch on his belt. We would see each other later in life and hook up but it wasn't the same that sixteenyear-old girl rush in my late twenties no longer was there. It was long over.

My crushed hurt from Red Caps dealings with the white girls had me wiling out. I remember coming up pregnant again honestly, I didn't know who the father was. I told Redcap it could be his or it could not be. I asked him what he was prepared to do. Redcap told me he would never look at the bastard. I knew that we were done but I didn't wanna give him no dear John letter while he was in jail. Selfsacrificing crap again.

While working at Churches Chicken, I met Jon he also worked there. We had grown fun of each other friends. There was no intent on moving forward in a relationship. I was in a destitute spot and needed a place to stay. Jon went to the jail as a courtesy with me to talk to Redcap about me moving into Jon's extra bedroom. We explained to Redcap there was nothing between us but room mating. He also reminded Redcap that I was damaged goods *pregnant*. I aborded the pregnancy doing what I thought was best. Jon protested stating he would have taken care of the baby while escorting me to the clinic to get the abortion making sure to announce to the people, he was not the father. After that experience I knew I would never do that again.

Jon had two kids who came to visit from time to time and my daughters also visited. Curiosity and many late-night friendly talks led me and Jon to intimacy. The night we decided to explore we were interrupted by a surprising knock at the door it was Redcap. Of all the dang nights to show up. Jon and I recovered pretty good putting things in order before opening the door. We were fast moving and had panicked pounding hearts. We didn't aim for that to happened it just did. Before the nights end, I explained to Redcap I was calling it quits and that night would be the last time he ever touched me. So, there I was for a bit living in the house with two men and five babies. Redcap found him a space in the tenderloin asking me to go with him My answer was no, and I stuck to it not because of Jon I was just finished with him. His lifestyle and declaration to keep selling dope and pimp white women was something I wasn't going to continue to swallow well especially after he quit his job.

Once I decide to be done, I am done, and I was done. He tried all kind of persuasive techniques especially with Jon's weakness for drugs. I once walked into the bar and found him and Jon sitting together, I turned right around and walked out and got back into my friends' car Bass and got dropped off at a church. Even though I had no understanding of *Holiness, or Hell* I knew I needed to pray and be in the house of the Lord.

Bass was this black supervisor I met while doing community service for GA he had taken a liking to me with his married self. I had always made it a practice to not sleep with another woman's husband that is bad Karma. When I hooked in the streets it was different, I found some married men who really just wanted to talk to somebody, funny enough about the love they had for their wife and then there were that other kind.

In any case Bass would show up at my work spot with flowers insisting that I let the other GA participants sweep the street and I hangout with him. I would tell him I was going to do my job. Bass would wait until I had swept for awhile and then he would lovingly insist I go with him. Bass would wine, dine, and introduce me to so many of his friends. He shot pool pretty good and of course I couldn't. Even as a teen it was never something I grasped but I could play the hell out of some pin pone, and we engaged in that together to. After some time, I did grow very fond of Bass. We did try to hook up sexually, but it was awkward. We did continue our friendship for years and he often helped me out of situations.

When Jon got home, I asked him what that was the

meeting at the bar with Redcap about. Jon told me Redcap offered him money and drugs to put me out of his house. He took the money and the drugs; I don't know if he agreed but he didn't put me out. Redcap then offered me money and sexual favors to return to him, but I had a made up my mind that I was done with him and that lifestyle. Redcap continued his adventures of in and out jailing. He told me he was going to Michigan to see his mom and asked if he could take the two baby daughters with him. It was always our agreement if it didn't workout to both share and take care of our children. He never sent the kids back. There were years and distance between me and my daughters. Until a judge finally granted me visitation for an Easter spring break. I as so sick and in the hospital during that Easter week my husband at the time Vince convinced Redcap to send the girls and he did. After that visit the girls and I found our way back to each other. You can read more in depth about that story in *Alice N Crackland*.

After many years the kids were grown, Redcap had gone back to his hometown married a woman that looked similar to his mother and settled down changing his ways. The two of them spent many years growing old together. Our baby daughter received a concern call Redcap was in the house alone after his sickly wife's children had taken his wife to live with them. Redcap was very stubborn as difficult as it was, he was convinced to return to California to live with my youngest daughter. Redcap was so headstrong and was participating in unsafe behaviors that eventually signaled that he needed care from assisted living for the safety of himself and others.

I was bringing the grandkids to see him quite regularly by then and continued to do so in his assisted living residence. The family had gotten accustomed to spending quite a bit of time engaging as a family weekly. Although I had some unresolved issues with Redcap regarding my children, I let it go for the sake of what is and the positive direction the family was headed toward. I didn't put my energy or focus much about how I felt about it I knew it was something that God wanted me to do.

One day he had the nerve to tell me that he was married, and he didn't want no romantic relationship with me. I had to remind him that I was not there for him if it had not been for the Lord, I would have cracked him in his head about my children and he knows why. I made sure he understood my visits were nothing more than platonic. I was here as transport for the grandchildren. I admit I checked his arrogant ignorance and nerve pretty tough in front of the grandchildren and I wasn't very nice about it. I almost felt sorry for him but let's not push it. I made sure he interacted with the grandchildren with arts and crafts, taking pictures, and sharing stories I wanted them to know something about their heritage.

We received a call from the hospital with their condolences Redcap had passed away with his wedding rings in his hands placed on his opened Koran. I believe he died of a broken heart. He no longer had communication with his wife, and she had developed dementia. He experienced hardship letting her go. I had compassion for him and was glad to know that someone had come into his life and made a loving difference. He saw the Glory of God in me.

My relationship with Jon increased and developed into a repetitive romantic world wind of drugs, nightmares, and fights. In six weeks, I was pregnant by him with our son quickly after abording the baby Redcap said he would never look at. Like other women I was vulnerable suffocating from my own childhood stuff men also experience this issue. Some people have a need to allow someone else to control their lives rather than them being able to do it themselves. *False safety zones*. Men have a way of spotting needy women it's part of their gift to pick the right bride but often used as an obscured entitlement. A woman is equipped with the gift of influence unfortunately we use it persuasively on ourselves to talk ourselves in and out of situations good or bad.

As time went on, Jon and I continued in our relationship of drug addiction, abuse, and the rearing of children. Two of the girls were with Redcap out of State at the time and my oldest daughter was with my aunt

Cedra. For some reason Aunt Cedra had surrendered my daughter to CPS This was something that puzzled me. Why would she do that? Per our agreement I had took my daughter to live with her until I found a place of my own. My son was little so he could stay with me at my cousin's house. Aunt Cedra took it a step further she called CPS to take my son . I was checking in with her daily and visiting so she knew exactly where to find me. There was a knock on my cousins' door we all including Jon were sitting around just talking. It was the police They said they got a report of abuse from a family member. I denied abusing him. I fed and changed him, and never left him with anyone else, even while I was getting high.

Finally, Jon said, "Hand him to me." It was a lot easier for me to hand him to Jon that to the police. But they took him anyway. I was humiliated, rejected and heartbroken again. There was no evidence nor legal reason for them to take my son. There was no immediate danger, no drugs or alcohol on the scene, no public disturbances nor search and seizure.

However, it was just that easy in the 80's to separate families it was the Government system form of genocide. Separation of black males from their wife and children, mothers from their children, and elders from their homes. As the crack addict adult children undersigned mortgages without their parents knowing causing them to lose their homes. It was brokenness, separation of the family unit, and trust. It had such a prevalent impact on our children's emotional and mental wealth, addiction of adults, and the black historical family as each understood its own were infringed.

I like many others felt like there was nothing I could do about it. So much anger welled up in me that I didn't know how to cope. I thought,

What's the use? My life is never going to change. All my kids are gone. Might as well get high. All thoughts of recovery were in the pipe. It became a "pipe dream." I spoke often about my children, but it was like a distant hope fading faster with every hit. I had the illusion that my children gave me focus and an identity as somebody important. I sank into depression and even heavier drug use.

My adventures came into play and eventually sent me to jail. I was in there enough time for Jon to make positive changes. Jon got involved with Glide Memorial Church and the *Facts on Crack* program. I must admit Jon was not an all-bad guy. He has many great characteristics and skills that often-got loss in the shuffle of addiction and his childhood trauma. He is a fabulous artist and his compassion for the community often leads to self-sabotaging choices that hurt him. He continues to bounce back and educate and grow his thought life. In fact, I must attribute two key factors of change in my life I got there by the way of Jon, The introduction of Glide Memorial Church and Shiloh Full Gospel Church. Jon was faithful to making changes at Glide and when I got released from jail, I followed suit. I It took time, but I changed my life and gained the custody of My daughter and son. I was an addict though. Jon had fell off the wagon and my story was I didn't want him to have to start all over by himself, so I fell off the wagon after him. "What a load of self-sabotaging and self-sacrificing crap."

All the trauma for both of us came rushing back yes, we had abstained from drug use, but the root of our hurt was not being addressed. When then issues surfaced, we struggled with that addiction and the violence between us. We eventually left Glide I was fired from my job there. I was glad for the support I had gotten but the teachings were hell bond. I knew in my Spirit there was more accountability for my actions and somehow, I had been called to come out. This led us to Shiloh Full Gospel Church the teaching bus driver's church who over many years grew to a Bishop and Prophet for the Lord. I had heard him testify on the Muni bus, but Jon somehow got hired to write scriptures on the church wall. I went to see if he was for real. I don't care what nobody says, "Jon is a Muslim to his heart." He has tracked himself to be connect to the tribe of Moors. I kept going back and back to that Church the word was spoken in me and gave me hope and life.

The final episode of abuse or shall I say when I got raccoon eyes from Jon took place on Egbert Street. That night I came in worn out from walking the streets. Work was scarce that night, and I didn't have much money or dope. I didn't really want to share the ten-shot I had, but I did. I went straight into the bedroom. Jon came in, and we took a hit on the pipe.

It wasn't enough to satisfy us both, but—just enough to get us edgy. I saw that Jon was "fiending," and even though I had just come in, I would have gone back out, but he didn't give me a chance. He started an argument and he seemed fired up already. I was sitting on the bed. I was not expecting what happened next. He straddled me and pinned my arms down with his knees, and he began beating me in my face mercilessly. I tried to fight him off, but I was pinned down. I just lay there crying and screaming. The nun had no soar in her.

The next morning, I woke up and it was dark. Then I realized my eyes were swollen shut. I was afraid to look in the mirror. I didn't want my kids to see me. I finally looked at myself in the mirror, and I broke out into tears. I had the eyes of a racoon. I heard my kids waking up so I ran to the couch and lay down and pulled the covers over my head. They came looking for me and they asked me why I had the covers over my head. I told them the truth—I had gotten beat up. They began to cry and at that moment I felt like the worse mother in the world.

I was feeling revengeful. I hadn't called the police on him, but I went to his friends' houses and showed them what he had done to me. I wanted everybody to see what kind of man he was. They all could see it but the problem was, I couldn't see it. I was in the kitchen cooking chicken, and I was holding a knife. Jon came in to confront me about showing my face to his friends. He came at me, but this time I drew the knife at him. I said I wasn't taking any more beatings. My uncle ran into the kitchen and got between us. He said that was enough. I put the knife down, and Jon left. I knew at that moment if I didn't do something, I would have to tell my son that I killed his father if he didn't kill me first. The relationship was over.

Now in regard to my son which is the best of Jon and me. He had never seen us function as a happy couple he was born and suddenly it was strife. He so desperately loved both of this so even though I had put Jon out my son would let him back in. I would wake up in the morning and Jon would be in the house. My proclamation of sorrowfulness is my choices in relationships but without them I would not have my flock.

Jon shadiness continued to grow and so did mine many ups and downs. I stopped working the streets, paying much more attention to my children, and healing in church. Jon and I still had bouts of arguments and episodes. Jon would go to jail, and I would take all those children to see him. He would act entitled talking to me harshly showing off in front of his jail inmates. The last time I visited him in jail with all the children we were all dressed in red and white to celebrate Valentine's Day which has always been my favorite holiday.

While Jon was doing his normal show out crap on me, I leaned over and ask the guard this is a contact visit correct. The guard responded with yes while nodding his head. I pulled my right arm and hand stretching it to an extended length and brought it quickly slamming a slap onto Jon's right jaw cheek and stated, "CONTACT," The jail roared with the laughter and approval of the visitors. I got up grabbed my babies and headed for the door. When arrived toward the outside a guard approached me stating, "Maam we could arrest you for that." I said, "good then maybe he can be the one out here taking care of the children and dealing with the hardships." The guard nodded and walked off.

During one of our arguments after Jon was out of jail and I had given my life gladly to the Lord Jesus. I remember Jon foaming at the mouth he wanted to hit me so bad, but the blood of Jesus had him bound he couldn't move. He told me when he left the house, he was walking down the street and some guy he didn't know punched him in his face so hard and he didn't know why. I call it an Earth Angel with a salvation warning. Touch not my anointed and do my profit no harm.

I remember it was a cloudy day and a teardrop fell from heaven and landed on my left eye in the very spot that was so tender to me. I knew it was a representation from the Lord that no man would physically strike me again. I was now under the Lord's protection. Then salvation was introduced to me, and I had given my life to the Lord Jon, and I got married.

Marie had a minster license and I believed I manipulated her into getting excited about it to perform the wedding ceremony between Jon and me. Since he did not make the arrangements, he was supposed to for a minster. I knew perfectly we she knew this was a mistake as well as my maid of honor who chose not to show. One of my friends from Glide Memorial came by to support me and I swear we were high and drunk this was the normality and homeostasis of surviving life with Jon during this season. My son has never seen us as a happy together couple but has grown to see us be civil in the same space with genuineness and respect.

My son has questions as an adult he has his abandonment issues and hurt from his childhood. I hope the answers can help to guide him further in his relationship, but I learned in my experience there's no answers for childhood traumas and generational curses. I had to find peace and a healing space in myself and changed my mindset. Therapy helped. I don't hold grudges from my childhood. I have made peace with my past. I can take accountability for yesterday but refused to be held hostage to the past nor do I allow anyone else to hold me hostage. I belong to the Lord all I can say is I'm so glad I'm not the same addict I was, and *Alice* has gotten herself some help. The conversation will be happening soon during one of his therapy sessions I have committed to family therapy with him. I'm hopeful rather than dreadful about our future session especially after he shared with me he learned what is it that a parent can tell you about the past that would make things better.

CHAPTER SIX

Another Man's Good Intentions

My interlude with Andy. He was someone Jon and met at Glide Memorial Church. We became very good friends; most people knew us and Andy as brother and sister. I usually told him about all my little secrets, and he was always comforting. Like me, Andy was on drugs, and we shared drugs together, but it wasn't the basis of our relationship. I used to see how he treated women, how he would go from one to the next.

Andy lived with us as many others in the early days. He also lived with me and the kids for Andy would cook, clean, and take care of the kids whenever I was out hustling, or I just wasn't home. I trusted him more than I trusted Jon, who was apparently fooling around with somebody because there were many days when he didn't come home. I remember when I found out he had moved in with another girl. I had learned this through my son. He took him for a night, but they spent it at the new girlfriend's house. My son came home and told me. I was angry, hurt, and I couldn't believe that Jon was such a coward that he would use our son for his dirty work. Out of pain and brokenness Andy tried to relieve my hurt which consist of a couple of sexually interludes. I ate the responsibility of desperate acts of despair and in that situation for dragging him into my self-loathing. We had announced our intent on marriage to others. Andy soon found a way to help us dissolve that catastrophe more about that in *Alice N Crackland*.

My prayer wishes are for those who need it get some help for trauma rather lose themselves in drugs, alcohol, and sex to cope. I certainly learned to do so. Black people during those days and even some now are not steered toward therapy there was and is so much stigma and reference to craziness and many labels. Liquor stores and dope was presented as the answer and ongoing relief just get high and forget about it, "here take a swig of this let it put some hair of your chest, smoke this, or do that, and/or a little nookie ain't never hurt nobody." Everything that was and is temporary but has lifelong negative effects and impact on self and family functioning. Jon went his way, Andy went his way, and me and the children went ours. I kept an ongoing relationship with Jon's two kids to which was shocking for him to find out so many years later.

My request to the judge was to take my name back and raise my son. I shared with the judge my concern Jon teaching my son violence. After many broken promises and it's your mama faults Jon left the Bay Area. Going forward he has returned and established relationship with his son. We now communicate well and have a great understanding our ourselves and downfalls. Jon learned to see God's glory in me, and I learned to respect the Glory that cradles him. As I get to the end of this chronologically recall accounts of *My Love was Blind*, I realize I was doing the same things as those loves I was angered by. I too was a cheater and could be abusive. Such as leading into the story below regarding my interlude with TU.

TU was a strange breed but, in my addiction, I tricklingly used him to get his money to wetnurse my crack addiction. Rather than trying someone new, I continued to search him down at his homemade treehouse built by him and set up as his forest residence. I knew this man had serious mental health issues. Why else would this man be living outdoors in jungle like home, in the early nineties, other than to escape the reality of his own pain. Homelessness had not surfaced to that magnitude during that time. But I worked him to make him think the magic happened even though it didn't, and he knew it and told me he was aware of my trickery.

In TU's defense perhaps, his death would have not occurred. I should've not been engaging with him in such a manner. It got complicated, he got possessive, and my spoken words became dangerous and deadly. I thought I was taking advantage of him hooking and crooking but my thoughts were proven to be incorrect. TU was emotionally strung out on me and made desperate attempts to control interactions with me and this caused me great distress. "I wasn't the kind of woman who handled distress well and there would be consequences." I thought my cleverness was to my advantage, but it turned out to be to my disadvantage. I had no control once the ball was rolled, over the possibility of what could and did happen. I often had warning signs of repeated cautions suggesting maybe I should rethink going down that road in search of that money hunt. I was a crazed addict in avoidance of my truths.

I can remember one day being enraged with TU's controlling attitude. I cautioned him not to test me, he continued to do so, and I threw gasoline on him. I threatened him with serious intent. If he didn't walk away and leave me alone, I was gonna light him up. I stood above him flicking the lighter from my bedroom window. That was a time of active bizarre behaviors. My brain and mind engaged in conflictual confused conversations, outrageous outburst, and I dabbled in doing vindictive stuff. I felt my anger justified my actions. I soon learned I had no authority to judge, do, or treat others in ways my sick mind and thoughts deemed. It also has had consequences and I got kids.

One day after a heated argument to get rid of TU I told him I would come by his space I was not going to at first, but my empty pocket calls of addiction were my guides, and I followed the lead. He was still acting neurotic after I located him. I tried to change my mind, but his wearisomeness kept at me. There was a Hispanic male policeman driving down the street at slow speed as I was urgently moving away from TU's controlling grasp TU was moving quickly toward me in aggressive frustration trying to verbally force me to spend time with him. Out of panicked fear I called out to the officer for help. I spoke the words to, TU, "if you don't stop f…ing with me you gone die." I had an awful feeling that I had made a mistake I should've not gone down there to mess with him. The officer drove near him asking him to go on about his business. TU became confrontational both verbal and physical with the policeman. He boldly walked in close proximity to the white van being driven by the officer. He was making derogatory statements and threats toward the policeman. This behavior drew the officer's attention from inside of the automobile to him getting out of the van. I was looking from afar I saw the officer draw his weapon and to my surprise, TU leapt at the officer and the gun went off. I wanted to run but I could not. My feet felt stuck, and all kind of thoughts were instantaneously shooting through my mind it was tragic! I was taken to the police station by a female officer who arrived at the scene. She asked me questions about the event. I was honest sharing the details of what I saw. I asked her what happened to TU. I learned he died I had an indescribable lump in my throat and shooting nervousness through my stomach. Although I didn't pull the trigger, I felt responsible for the outcome in the shot fired. May he rest in paradise, I knew that the if I did not give my life to the Lord Jesus, I was going to die, "it was undeniable there was blood on my hands, to the Glory of God salvation came for me."

Now this is why I called it *sheltering*. God always knew my downfalls and self-sacrificing attempts looking for a way out because I thought I wasn't deserving of his love. He showed it to me anyway. This drew me closer to him and I hate to disappoint God in thought or deeds. I fall short! I call on him to help me, not work passively, but actively on change; "I truly do want to transition for the better of what is spoken to my spirit, regarding God's envisions for me, walking in the calling and fulfilling my chosen purpose according to the measure he has given to my charge. Thank You, Jesus!

CHAPTER SEVEN

Conciliation with Loved Ones

I had two recent reconciliations one being spiritual and the other family. I learned much about myself by just listening to the conversations in my environment. Marriage and my spiritual partnerships are not for sale doing so does not allow appropriate friendship development or spiritual growth. I'll be speaking more regarding spiritual partnerships in the *Book of Testimonies* published by the end of 2021. However, it is important to me to leave you the reader with this, "the ground is level at the cross there are no big I's or little U's in Christ Jesus." He does not play favoritism or care more about one of his children versus another whether they are a beggar or a Prophet, no hierarchy all fall short of the Glory of God, and all are called to repentance. We are precious in his eyesight especially those who belong to him. He labors long with us and our answer to his call.

During this general family conversation what boys are taught versus girls' everyone there weighed in. My daughter to be Nessa shared her concern of girls being taught body Shaming, Catholicism, and purity of oneself and the boys got another message. She shared about herself and mother leaning past those intimidating shaming teachings not to love yourself and body and their climb to silent liberality in appreciating themselves. My Daughter Dosh asked what was used to measure to judge success in self-acceptance and the rights and wrongs of what boys are taught versus what girls regarding their sexuality and life's choices the dos and don'ts? Men being taught to soar their wild oats ad girls not to like or appreciate sex or her wild Oats not equally important. It's one-sided setting men up to cheat and women to except it.

The message has two be the same in order for it to balance equally in future marriage. Our agreement is both boys and girls should receive the same message. My son Zeus said, "everybody has their weight to lift but weight don't build muscle resistance does. For dessert we had a live testimony one of Zeus old friends and students came by. Zeus has a loyal friendship base of friends that trust and admire him and his wisdom. His friend shared his relationship troubles. Little did he know he was in the room with two social workers and a marriage & family therapist. I respected this man's ability to lay himself bear. It was a night filled with laughter, unraveling relationship topic conversation. We were all able to learn and grow. It felt like as a team we all recognized we are so busy dealing with our own trauma we wear it as our badge of safety. In our own delusional confusion, we unconsciously bring those feelings of abandonment and childhood experiences into our intimate interactions with others with an expectation that they know they exist and are intentionally trying to hurt us. The truth is sometimes this is true people are aware of their partners weakness and vulnerabilities. However, their own trauma exposition is a deterrent. There are heart wounds to bear when thirst and hastiness are the foundation of relationships.

I had a conversation with Rach, one of the authors in this book and great longtime friend. I had an opportunity to digest and finally process my feelings of not been in search but my backwards thinking had been at play. I have struggled in loneliness before, during, and post COVID. I believed that somehow my relief of this loneliness would come from a physical male presence in my life.

God pointed out to me that he has been here the whole time through all the failed loves, and he's lifted me from every one of those disappointments and failures.

All these years I thought I had been waiting for *The Brides Promise* it's my second book sank unto *Alice N Crackland* revision and the husband I wait for referred to as Boaz. The more me and Rach talked the revelation jumped in my spirit I had to take a seat. The Lord revealed in all of the relationships I've had with men there was none like Him and he was not like a man. His love has nothing to do with the masculine sense of love. I had so much disappointment in spousal relationships, and I appeared to be anxious to get into another because it had been a long time according to my calendar. No earthly husband could ever stand in the place of my God. Lord has proven himself to be a jealous God in my life. He has made it known . He doesn't like the idea of my thoughts that man is better suited to take care of me than Him. I gained the reality of my faulty thoughts. No way I can depend on a man to be the source of my all. That's old news. I can only account my backwards thinking to the trauma of masculinity falseness. I got confused and I have to be careful because words have power and the ability to stagnate or progress what's in store for my promise. I had blocked my Boaz from appearing. I was blinded by my thoughts and experiences with man regarding love. Now with corrected understanding I acknowledge God has been here for me from the cradle to this present day showing me his love even when I reject it. I know parts of this about God's love reads like a quote or cliché. I believed it although my actions didn't demonstrate it. I now understand through this revelation I have had the *Brides Promise* the whole time and I was not even aware of it.

What I want people to know about me is that my bedroom door is closed. It is my desire to wait for my portion in all things with the guidance of the Lord. I am an open book for safety for those in need. I'm in a place of non-judgment sometimes I might not react in a way that is inappropriate and I'm working on that, but my heart is to do the right thing. My response reactions are connected to the caring, past hurts, and the road ahead to victory in supporting my family, friends, and community. My task regarding relationships is to STOP and do the work to get to know somebody. It's important to see a potential suitors' actions in the different seasons that arrive like hardship, death, angriness, jealousy, and remember this list can get longer according to your lifestyle and needs. I say "take him to your mama house and have him put up a tent and see what kind of juice seeps out the pressed grape.

CHAPTER EIGHT

Suitor's Checklist

Pen & pad moment! Mama, Marie used to tell me I dated men who were unavailable, and I thought somehow, she was insulting me until I took a great look at my dating pattern saved and unsaved. These attention seeking behaviors, therefore, extending my existence in lost superficial relationships of self-defeat and broken pieces of me lying naked bared to the universe. It took me a lifetime to figure out the meaning of Mommie dearest statements unavailable meant. "Whatever did she mean? I saw these guys and talked to them on the phone." Some were intimate relationships, some I lay chase to and then it was those I ran from, even they were not available. I learned availability had another meaning besides picking up the phone to say hello. I am most appreciative for the motherly advice. She would be proud I finally grasped the concept and hopeful of it's use in my life. It took me a few times to implement some of her teachings.

I always hear people say, "Follow your heart." That is the worst advice to ever give anyone. The heart can be wicked, cunning, and often is led by the desires of your flesh. The statement should be, "Follow the One that lives in your heart." I know that you can't focus on externals, but you need to do a checklist. Remember about *rules*— they apply in every part of your life. Use them!

Believe me, I am down with romance, marriage, love, and all that, but there is something more that is needed for a lasting RELATIONSHIP/ MARRIAGE. There is an order to the universe, as Marie says. We women are out of order because we have switched roles. God has set high standards for us. It shows in the way He loves us unconditionally, takes care of us, forgives us, protects us, and provides for us. He is the head of our lives. When we get married, our husband becomes the head of our house, but God is the Head of both of our lives. Our husband takes on the responsibility as our protector, provider, and all the rest with the provisions of God.

Here is where the checklist comes in. If a man asks you to marry him, can he fulfil the basic obligations of a husband? Is he a man of God? Does he tithe? Does he have a job? We know not all men have jobs. If not, tell him to come back courting when he does. Is he generous with more than just his sperm? How many baby-mamas does he have? And how many babies? This will give you an indication of how faithful or unfaithful he will be or if child support for his adult children will be drawn from your tax returns. Is he supporting his children? Ask yourself if you're willing to raise his other children or pay what he failed to pay. If not, warning! Red Flags! Do not approach Go. Flee! Now there are some men who don't have these particular situations but have commitment issues which is a part of that unavailable theory. Just in case you missed it reader don't have room for my love in their lives you have to prod them for realness not false attention.

Other important considerations are his finances, his family background, and how he copes with good and bad decisions. What is his bounce back after he loses a loved one, job, and don't get his way? Does he have a history of violence? A criminal history? Or is he on drugs? Or is he bisexual? It is of the most important to put him in the firring pan. These things are predictors of what's to come, and it ain't always pretty when ignored. You will catch hell unless he has been reborn Remember the tent observe his behavior it will show you a lot about how he handles conflict and solidify solutions or crumbles. No woman can change a man before or after marriage. Your love, your sex, and your babies will not change his character or his habits. This is something only God can do. Before you marry, let God finish His job. In the end, you will know if this man should be your husband. God will show you everything. We choose to ignore the warning signs, because we don't want to be alone or live in our imagination. Here is an analogy fall in love with a guy because of that curly swirl of hair that fail on his forehead. He wasn't even nice to you but oh the attraction! Now four babies later you don't like him, and he can't stand you and he is bald, the swirl curl is gone. We also expect thoughts of our love will overcome all obstacles. Sooner or later, the very warning signs you ignored surface, and the truth is out. You knew it but didn't want to see it. Then you're stuck!

This leads me to talk about Bighunk, Elder Teach, and Da Pasta, Now with Bighunk I had finally been healed of my fear of huge men taller and bigger than myself. I spoke earlier in the book about watching my mom get beaten down and those feelings of fear of dark and tall men towering. I was introduced to Bighunk during the days I room-mated in Richmond an spent some evening outs. He interests me because of various reasons stated above but he was aggressive and lacked the ability to engage appropriately and lovingly. He did some chance begging and I kept him afloat engaging him romantically while I was traveling but I knew that it would never work because he did not possess the intimacy or equipment skills for a commitment.

Now Elder Teach, I had no attraction to him at all I believe God had me on assignment but sometimes I get caught up in away. I shouldn't by allowing my menace to get colluded in. Rejection has always been a root from my childhood when those feelings arise it can trigger the little girl Alice in me. Elder Teach was a minster who had a seizure and had difficulty adjusting back to the universe. He would stand there with that blank stare as if he was in another world. My assignment was to innocently brush by Elder Teach and remind him of God's earthly pleasures in life. A snap back. Of course, this is a back reflection. I did not recognize the intensity or the exactness of the assignment as usual until it had ended. Recalling Marie, also known as my Rebe and my backwards thinking without-doubt a raised hand to the truth. He woke up from his mental slumber with the fire from heaven preaching and praying. I believe what captured my attention was the word of God. I loved hearing the word. But I observed him becoming more finger pointed, blameful, and judgmental criticism of others during prayer. He was narcissistic and was very contradictory like offering and then retracting angrily his offers as if he did not suggest. "Did I mention stingy. He grew to act as if he was better than me and he would never bless me with his attention. This triggered my alter character Chickee. I sought to teach him a lesson and so I did. He was got! Then while I was gardening the Lord suddenly came upon me and shared with me my misuse of the assignment. It was revealed to me that I pursued Elder Teach out of my feelings of rejection and not because I cared for him. I was hit with the two-edge sword of God's cut and healing. To show myself approved by God's revelation of me I went to Elder Teach and shared with him he made me feel less than and that he was better than me so I intentionally pursued him to show him that I could get him if I wanted, and so I did but I apologize because it was not Christ like. He was both stunned and silenced.

Let's not forget Da Pasta, the juice he was like a communion cup filled with Kool-Aid and stale crackers that chocked a girl. After many months of toddling back and forth I decided to change worship spots but soon had to return. First of all, I want to say there is nothing wrong about having interest in a single man and you are single, but he still can be unavailable La Wanda. The skirt chaser was revealed to me. This man had a very subtle way of pulling women in unnoticed by anyone else as if you were a desired secret. I can admit my attraction to him especially because of the cleverness of how he used the word of God. Lust encouraged me to look right pass the truth in my face until God forced my eyes open to not only see but understand the spiritual sickness and damage that was occurring. I once heard him ask his baby mama who out of wedlock bore him a son why she left him and the church after having his baby because she was his biggest supporter. I thought to myself how rude he was for shaming her no offer of marriage from the preacher what a reduction. I couldn't figure out how he thought she was his biggest supporter and didn't rebuke the sexual advances. I mean no judgment by this, but some men can be so insensitive. He had no real care for women but to use them categorically as he saw fit. I saw him, Da Pasta and his gang of preachers, and deacons standing on the alter during praise and worship checking out the women, shrugging shoulders, pointing fingers, and cracking jokes. I told myself I am outta here and not because he did not openly show his pretensions feelings for me, but his coat tail had been pulled. I confess I've taken more than a few falls since salvation, and these are the reasons I've learned to be still in my flesh and allow God to do the choosing. I was very giving of myself the cooking, tithing, and genuineness but it was not of God.

CHAPTER NINE

Reminiscing, Lingered Heart Ache Widow

Icould not quite understand the sorrowfulness that I was feeling. As picture of Vince flashed on my phone it was August nineth the date, he was pronounced dead over ten years ago. I understood what was happening on the inside of me. There was a sense of sadness, but growth was occurring. I found it important to understand my patterns and triggers to help with forward movement, particularly those emotional hot buttons that possess the potential to ignite and invitation to undesirable familiar spirits or lysing moments. Sometimes I wonder was it easier when I was ignorant living in pretentious sleepiness with an unknowingly disregard of truth. Now that I have been awaken from some old and backwards thoughts, I am accountable to share the good news. Jesus is still in the salvation business.

I can't see the full scope, but I'm putting the effort in to clean the plank, out of my eyes and allow God to create a righteous spirit within me. Over the years deeper thoughts of what God has done for me shines a revealing light into the nature of my soul. I can agree without excuses of what he has shown me about me. He has established that He is the "GREAT I AM!" And because of who He is and what

He's done, I am getting those relatable lessons on who I am and whom I belong to. I am part of the system that is teaching me away to flourish and contribute to a different kind of security in Christ and my salvation and women of God as a whole person. No more husband church shopping, harnessed obtained leashes, hoof mouth busy body in fornication, and living out of the desire of a want rather than a need.

I can testify and give witness to God not putting more on me than I could bear. Sometimes I am just not aware that He has provided. I can be slow in recognizing what collection of tools, skills, and provisions were deposited for me to Glorify him and better my situation. I tend to get revelation in pieces not in chunks. "Once I get it, I go to it!" Then I look for the open door, window, an/or signs and wonders to assist me to fall in line, apply the knowledge. Now I'm getting in step with my universal aurora of mind, body, spirit , and soul connected to God's spirit and the purpose of my existence. That doesn't mean the mountain changes or Lucky charms appears suddenly and all is worked out. Sometimes relief is delayed, but mindset and faith engulf the metaphoric power to impact immediate transitions upon belief before change occurs. Gratefully so! The Lord has made a way of escape for me, and I choose to take it. "If I should fall and I do and have often, I get up and keep going!" I hope you do as well reader if not start.

Here I am bare and naked, palpitating as I share the revelation of my true love story. Living in silent grief of what I lost but not what I have gained. Yesterday has no redo's, nor takeback's or shoulda coulda's. My heart has held space of captivity far too long, ghosted blocking my ability to connect in the universe to my husband to be. I must admit Vince told me. Not when I asked him during those long settings on treasure

Island in the back of the limo but with his mannerism, he had a way of speaking to me and letting me know things indirectly. It's a perplexing flashback with him I experienced deeper emotional wounds with Vince than any of my other fist-punch lovers. The loss of our relationship was like a dagger thrusted into my heart a violation of trust and understanding. He broke up the triangle threesome we shared with God. Those words he spoke to me played repeatedly in my head for years. "Your next husband...., and soon I'm going to punish you." With my dampened eyelashes I no longer want to be the lingering widowed martyr of marriage.

As time progressed over the years Vince, saw me in God's glory. My slogan to him was, "from Jesus I came and to Jesus I shall return." He taught me many things. Such as compassion, forgiveness, and especially not to have an expectation that he would hit me. Vince once raised his hand, it appeared to be coming toward me from my perspective as fear and my reaction was guarded. It was a pure natural instinct, a product from my past experiences. Vince was so apologetic and assured me that was not his intent. He stated, "I would never he do such a thing. I was merely reaching for you." With my whole heart I was compelled to believe him.

Over the years, he was so attentive to me and the children. I learned to trust him around my daughter's. I observed him as he interacted with them. I noticed when speaking with them he would look them in their eyes and not their bodies. If they were wearing something inappropriate, he would gently assert his dissatisfaction in their choice of wardrobe. He loved and cared for them as well as my son and all the other neighborhood children as if they were his own.

But the reality is like all the rest, he also cheated on me it was like a sweet-and-sour crudeness. He became cold and distant. His rejection combined with adultery became unbearable for me. After all rejection has its limits. if a man leaves me unattended, eventually I lose attraction. I got needs to. Those old thoughts surfaced but I never cheated on him. I realize reader I had grown. I became weary being married but living single. This kind of Love was not enough to sustain my feelings of rejection and trauma conspired urgers, while he transported the limo riders and is his lovers through the bay area. Regretful for the upcoming loss and grief to come I packed his suitcase. You can read more about this story in detail in my book *Alice N Crackland.*

Let's call him Bobble head, I found this guy on an online dating website and begin to talk to him more regularly, met with him and hung out. I don't like dating websites people online catfish lying about who they are and what they do. How is the lie going to line up to truth when you make a connection? But here it is. Bobble head seem like a nice enough guy. I spent time with him and his family in Sacramento we had fun times and the intimacy was good. In the short version I manipulated the situation further to us moving in together. It was time for me to transition. I thought it could possibly work it was a quick onset. He is a believer and did attend church on his own and with me. Marie liked him to she thought he had some potential. She was shocked when I start telling her he was still on dating websites engaging with other women and to me that is still cheating. I told her and him he was too old for that and guys his age knew the dating rules, don't obey the rules and act like young boys. Bishop Lee even liked him. I drank wine and sometimes something stronger but as it turned out Bobble Head didn't have a consistent job and was a drunk, I never had much patience for drunkards. In my crack addiction I only drank so that I could come down to take hits of crack and go back up again.

I took him to a family function mind you reader; my family is a hard crew they will make jokes and talk about you especially given the right circumstances. Bobble Head was spilling drinks sloppy drunk falling and had to take a nap. It was embarrassing for me even if it wasn't for him. He also had proclaimed an ex-wife status that was actually not an ex but still very much married and she started showing up. I learned this after Bobble Head, and I moved in together the two of them had still been living in the same house together previously. She had a man, and their problems soon became our problems. I don't know what happened to her boyfriend. Oh Lord what had I gotten myself in. I was planning my exit.

Once we had a seven AM morning appointment I went to the store and by the time I got back he was drunk a friend of his stopped by and he drank beer. When I returned, "dude you drunk?" and friend says oh it's my fault. I spoke. " How can it be your fault he's a grown man he's aware of our plans?" I knew then the urgency of the situation there was no pretending. I could not stay and would not stay. I packed my stuff over a time placing it in storage. I told him my deadline date and advised him to tell his wife to stay out of my way until I was gone for her safety and my salvation. I found a place, I couldn't take it anymore. We had one more lustful goodbye night together. I called one of my favorite nieces she helped me pack up my truck and we were gone heading into my new sunset. His wife showed up to I guess she wanted to see me off. I'm really kind of proud of myself that lying moment was disguised but I was not ignorant of it. It lived a shorter lifespan. The issue with Bobble Head is disloyalty and maybe because of his hurt in his previous experience of a cheating wife. I would like to leave this section as a tell all when you're dating someone do not be so disheartening give your all and receive it all.

Let's call him Chicago. On one of my trips to see my family in the Lou I planned to drive four hours to Chicago to see Chicago. I 've known this Belize Cat many years and grew to adore his wisdom and gentleness. I couldn't recollect where I had met him, but he told me he was a transportation driver on a bus. We somehow changed information and established communication regularly. I feel like Chicago is the one guy I have ever met that sees the Alice in me and knows how to nurture her growth in such a gentleness. In all fairness I believe his true intent was to coach me into my full potential but not as my lover. I always say he is the one who got away. I don't believe I have ever had that feeling for a man. Our friendship was clearly platonic at first and it was my intent to keep it that way. I only paid attention to his voice on the phone and shared so much of the real me. This went on and I benefited from it greatly. His phone attention was a place of safety for me. I knew that I had special feelings for Chicago, but I could keep them hidden and enjoy the spiritual release maybe one day it could be more. Then I learned he was leaving California my potential more would be lost if I did not act with some sense of urgency. We made a connection the night before he left and to the wee hours of the morning with fine wine, snacks, and great company. We continued a friendship but there are thousands of roads and miles between us. Excitedly I took the four-hour drive to see Chicago. He put effort into finding and paying for our lodging. It was beautiful. I remember we were having breakfast and I was on my way to the bathroom I leaned over and kissed him on the top of his smooth bald head as I headed for the restroom. An elderly white woman stopped me and said, " now I want you to always remember that" meaning kissing him on his head. I smelled my intent of hopefulness that I would not only remember it but do it more often. Although my clear openly intent was sex. It was the first time in my life, I had experienced such non-sexual intimacy and felt honestly cared for as a woman. It wasn't for the lack of trying. At first, I took it as rejection, but I knew that was a lie, it not happening was actually for my protection. My understanding grew as he shared deeper parts of himself with me.

Before I left Chicago, I told Chicago that I loved him. It might have been a mistake to launch out into the deep, but the chapter of what ifs needs closing. It felt like six months after that "I Love you" statement we had no communication. I had my wounded pride, and he probably didn't know what to do with that. I'm thankful we made contact and are friends. I understand My needs or more than he can provide for me and accept it. Chicago had his own life plan that I selfishly interrupted when he was taking flight from Oakland. He is right a woman does need balance in her life. It's like Adele's song, "hello on the other side! So, to my surprise a year later I get a ring in the evening, and it is Chicago. Nervously I shooshed the conversations in the room swallowed my throat and answered cheerfully. My heart, beat with anxiety to hear the words he would speak on the other side of that phone. His voice was pleasant and drawing as usual and I could not deny the flush in my spirit and face as we talked. Chicago shared with me he was not in a great emotional head space during my visit, to Chicago but he appreciated me coming and he felt better after my being there with him. He thanked me for just being me. Now earlier I had prayed with My sister in Christ Stephanie, and I found her prayer to be strange seeming I had no idea what she was talking about but knew it was relevant because I know her. She said soon you are going to be released from something and then she prayed about a him and I was like who is him in my mind? Chicago sharing with me released me from the feelings I had of rejection and thoughts of that trip. I knew then and know now that there is a special connection between the two of us.

In closing Pen & pad moment! This may not be necessarily a relationship but it something one might desire as well. My desire is to be married again. Although I want intimacy, I am now aware it has taken what I believed was a long time. But the more I have learned about myself and utilizing this knowledge, *I may be damaged goods, but a rising star in the making.*

My pattern of impatience saved or not in relationship status was all too familiar and literary similar in nature. Loneliness creating a lying moment that could lead to desperate acts of affection and nextday sorrow or another pitstop relationship. If the only intimate connection to someone else is to feel whole, then pieces are broken.

I had to learn to be comfortable with myself by taking myself out to dinner, clubbing, and all kind of events. I am solo. I have the choice to go and come as I please. I had to create rituals of giving myself love and appreciation and truly making sense of what that meant for me. In my past relationships I felt together, as couples there was no way neither of us pulled our weight in the relationship. If one is still judging others and themself, "nun tin ain't ben learnt." This is a major ingredient to blinded love situations perhaps coupled with black eyes. In a intimate partner violence situation either party has the capacity to throw hands. This expression is not an excuse or even a cool factor neither is it something I heard is something I know. One thing I do no without doubt my life's experienced circumstances and the grace of God I would not be the black-eyed queen that I am. So, I gladly share my testimony in hopes of a better me and a better you reader.

ABOUT THE AUTHOR

L a Wanda Marrero is an author, poet, mother and grandmother, missionary, community advocate for life insurance awareness, and Associate Marriage & Family clinician. She is the founder of the Adnawal Inc. (nonprofit), promoting family health and wellness, physically, emotionally, and mentally. She works through community collaborative partnerships and services for seniors, adults, and youth. She created a therapeutic writing class called "Start Steppin." After publishing *Alice N Crackland* in 2008, she realized her writing was an essential tool in acknowledging and accepting and overcoming challenges that she faced as a child. She thought others could also benefit from learning to express themselves through the art of writing and pretense. It's within her understanding that her past addictions and actions impacted many lives. The Lord's grace is her redemption road, *a bridge to healing.* Having *firsthand knowledge* of dysfunctional family dynamics has become her motivating passion to become licensed in her above chosen fields. She recently opened Unstoppable Publishing Company to give others an opportunity to store their experiences in between the covered pages making room for the new. She has co-authored several books such as *Unstoppable, When the Vow Breaks, Mounted Wings Beyond What I See, Blinded love, Testimonies Whole Again,* the publication of her mother's book, *Marie's Treasure Chest, My Love was Blind* and a host of other evolving projects. Over the years she has grown in the skills of coaching, editing, ghostwriting, and BBS certified therapist Sound mind makes sound choices. Her services in these areas are for hire.

Contact <u>unstoppablepublishingcomp@gmail.com</u> .

Phone no: *5105935367*

"Don't delay! I can help you turn that journal, memo, or idea into your book!

Milton Keynes UK
Ingram Content Group UK Ltd.
UKHW021221100324
439016UK00007B/125